Pocket Change

PITCHING IN FOR A BETTER WORLD

MICHELLE MULDER

ORCA BOOK PUBLISHERS

Library and Archives Canada Cataloguing in Publication

Mulder, Michelle, 1976-, author
Pocket change : pitching in for a better world / Michelle Mulder.
(Orca footprints)

Includes bibliographical references and index.
Issued in print and electronic formats.
ISBN 978-1-4598-0966-6 (hardcover).—ISBN 978-1-4598-0967-3 (pdf).—
ISBN 978-1-4598-0968-0 (epub)

1. Consumption (Economics)—Environmental aspects—Juvenile literature. 2. Consumption (Economics)—Social aspects—Juvenile literature. I. Title. II. Series: Orca footprints

HC79.C6M384 2016   j339.4'7   c2016-900771-5
          c2016-900772-3

First published in the United States, 2016
Library of Congress Control Number: 2016931889

Summary: Part of the nonfiction Footprints series for middle readers, with color photographs throughout. Readers will learn how purchases affect the environment and what the world would look like if we bought less stuff.

Orca Book Publishers is dedicated to preserving the environment and has printed this book on Forest Stewardship Council® certified paper.

Orca Book Publishers gratefully acknowledges the support for its publishing programs provided by the following agencies: the Government of Canada through the Canada Book Fund and the Canada Council for the Arts, and the Province of British Columbia through the BC Arts Council and the Book Publishing Tax Credit.

Cover images by Getty Images, Shari Nakagawa
Back cover images (top left to right): Fallen Fruit (David Burns and Austin Young), Kiva, Helder Ramos; (bottom left to right): William Neumann Photography, Katie Stagliano, William Neumann Photography

Design and production by Teresa Bubela and Jenn Playford

ORCA BOOK PUBLISHERS
www.orcabook.com

Printed and bound in Canada.

19 18 17 16 • 4 3 2 1

Nomadic families, like this one in Morocco, carry all their belongings with them. That's a good reason to keep shopping to a minimum! VLADIMIR MELNIK/DREAMSTIME.COM

For Chris, Susannah and Mark.

Contents

CHAPTER THREE:
FEELING LIKE A MILLION BUCKS

CHAPTER FOUR:
NOW THAT'S RICH

Introduction

On a summer evening, my family loves gardening in our parking spot—especially because neighbors always come by to chat.
GASTON CASTANO

Have you ever walked along the shampoo aisle in a drugstore and wondered which bottle to choose? You're not alone. It's often hard to know which product to spend your money on.

Over the years, I've lived in small places where stores offered very few options. When I ran out of shampoo in Peru, for example, I bought the only kind sold in the village shop. When I returned to Canada, I felt completely overwhelmed the moment I walked into a store. So many things to choose from! And so few that I really needed. Years later, I wondered how our purchases affect the environment. Factories use Earth's resources to create products, and when we don't want an item anymore, we often toss it into the landfill. How would the world look if we bought less stuff?

Lately, I've been reading about creative ways that people meet their needs without buying much at all. It's all about community. Did you know that if you want a blender in Toronto, Ontario, you can borrow one from the Kitchen Library? Or that in Kenya, families share a small amount of money—sometimes less than twenty-five dollars—to start entire businesses? And strong communities aren't just fun to live in. They're good for the environment and can reduce poverty too. How? Grab a friend and a snack to share, come along and find out!

Do we really need so many options? PINDIYATH100/DREAMSTIME.COM

My Two Cents' Worth

In university, my dormitory room looked out onto this cherry tree.
ELLEN GONELLA

My university dorm room was tiny. I didn't have my own kitchen or bathroom, and I loved it! Sharing space meant great conversations in the cafeteria, and drinking hot chocolate with housemates in the living room down the hall. These days, I sometimes joke that our apartment building reminds me of my university dorm, and I mean that in a good way!

CHAPTER ONE

Pssst! Don't Tell Anyone!

SHOPPING? HOW EMBARRASSING!

Did you know that, until a few hundred years ago, buying a loaf of bread could start terrible rumors? Usually, rural women made all their bread at home, and if neighbors saw a woman buying it, they might whisper that she was too lazy to bake or that her bread was like a stone. Until the 1800s, families proudly made most of the things they needed to survive. Now, in many cultures, families buy as much as they can. How did we go from being embarrassed to shop to being proud of it?

It's a long story. And it started hundreds of thousands of years ago, when humans first walked the Earth.

PACK IT OR TOSS IT?

Human beings, or *Homo sapiens* as scientists call us, have existed for more than 200,000 years. And for 99 percent of that time, we've wandered around, following our food. If sweet red berries

Fingers crossed that the bread will turn out well; otherwise people will start whispering about this 15th-century French woman!
A.DAGLI ORTI/BRIDGEMAN IMAGES

These days, so many people love shopping that malls like Galeries Lafayette in Paris have become tourist destinations.
T.W. VAN URK/DREAMSTIME.COM

grew in the valley in summer, we were there to pick them, and if antelope ran across the plains in the fall, we showed up to nab some juicy steaks. As soon as food ran out in one place, we moved on to the next, carrying everything we owned on our backs. Even if wide-screen TVs had existed, no one would have wanted one. Imagine carrying it around day after day!

MONEY IN OUR POCKETS

About 12,000 years ago, people in the Near East (western Asia) began to help nature along a bit. When they found a plant they liked, they cleared space for it and brought water from the nearest lake or river. The plants grew bigger and yielded more food. Eventually, families stopped following their food around and stayed in one place, planting and tending their crops.

Of course, people couldn't grow everything they needed. So they traded what they had for what they wanted. That was often trickier than it sounds. A family wanting to bake bread

This is a fei stone, traditional currency on the island of Yap in the South Pacific. One stone could weigh as much as a small car!
ERIC GUINTHER/GFDL/WIKIMEDIA.ORG

No need for money at this market in Lembata, Indonesia: People swap what they have for what they want, from corn to whale meat. JEFFREY NORTHEY

could offer a cow to a wheat-growing family, but if the wheat growers didn't want a cow, they were all stuck. And that's why our ancestors invented money.

Strictly speaking, money isn't the stuff you hold in your hand when you go to the store for an ice-cream bar. It's the idea that an object (a coin, a bill, a plastic card) can represent how much something is worth. The objects are called *currency*. Long ago, some societies used salt, spices or sugar as currency. They were valuable because people used them for cooking. But this kind of currency was hard to carry around in large quantities, and an unexpected rainstorm could dissolve a family's life savings! About 5,000 years ago, folks in the Americas, Asia, Africa and Australia began using shells to represent how much something was worth. They were light, durable and waterproof, and as long as people agreed that they were valuable, they worked very well as a currency. These days, most countries use metal circles (coins) and paper rectangles (bills) as currency. And many people use plastic cards to represent the metal and paper, but more about that later. Whatever it's made of, money is powerful stuff.

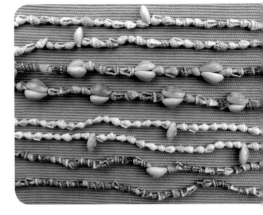

These days, we use coins or bills as currency, but people have used everything from cows to cowry shells. VICKYRU/ISTOCK

WORK? NAH...

Making everything by hand, like our ancestors did, took a lot of time. It's easy to imagine families hundreds of years ago working far harder than we do today. But did you know that people in North America now work more hours than ever before? Historians say that until the late 1700s, most people worked just a few hours each day. Usually they worked together, helping each other bake bread, spin wool, build houses and barns, and harvest crops. They spent the rest of their time relaxing with family and friends, eating, telling stories or making music. Unfortunately, life was unpredictable. Bad weather, plant diseases or insects could destroy crops from one

When this family built a barn in Redwater, AB, family, friends and neighbors all lent a hand (or two). NA-2497-6/GLENBOW.ORG

day to the next. Families that had enough to eat one year might starve the next.

Then, in 1769, an invention by James Watt of Scotland changed everything. He developed the steam engine to pump water out of flooded coal mines, but businessmen quickly realized that the engine could power cloth-making machines and sewing machines. Soon clothing factories began springing up across Europe, and word spread that factory workers earned regular paychecks. Parents in the countryside loved the idea of earning a steady income (without the aggravation of bad weather or insects), and many families packed up and headed to the cities so adults and children alike could work in factories.

The big buildings were noisy, smelly, dark and dangerous, and since factory owners paid for each piece of clothing worked on, families figured out how much money they needed and only worked enough to earn that amount. At first, their bosses

For these kids in Georgia, United States, in 1909, climbing onto machinery was part of their job. This was one of many photographs by Lewis Hine that helped change US labor laws. NATIONAL ARCHIVES PHOTO NO. 03-0317M

offered them more money so that they would work more, but workers preferred to spend time with their families. Eventually, factory owners came up with a solution that would keep their factories running smoothly: they started paying workers *less* so that they had to work more to survive!

SHARE...OR ELSE!

Soon business owners in North America and Europe were opening factories that made everything from cutlery to bicycle parts. And city folk (who had little time to make their own clothes, furniture and other household items) got used to buying factory-made items. Shopping wasn't embarrassing anymore. It was a way of life.

Not everyone agreed with all this shopping though. In 1848, German philosophers Karl Marx and Friedrich Engels wrote *The Communist Manifesto.* The book insisted that buying things isn't the road to happiness. Marx and Engels believed that folks would eventually realize this and choose to share everything instead. In 1917, Russia tried to leap right into that predicted happy future. New laws declared that the government would divide all money, food and resources equally between people. Unfortunately, the people doing the dividing often put aside extra for themselves, and soon the people in power had plenty, and the rest were very poor. Communism has had similar results in several countries around the world. So far, there's no proof that forcing citizens to share makes anyone happier than before—especially when the leaders themselves aren't so good at sharing!

PLEASE, PLEASE, PLEASE SHOP

While communists disapproved of North America's and Europe's shopping, others longed to enjoy the same opportunities.

The guys in the back, Friedrich Engels (l) and Karl Marx (r), wrote The Communist Manifesto *in 1848. Think they knew their book would change the world?* ROGER-VIOLLET, PARIS/ BRIDGEMAN IMAGES

Before planned obsolescence, automobile designer Henry Ford joked that people could buy cars in any color they liked as long as it was black. NA-1824-1/GLENBOW.ORG

Before television, posters were one of the best ways to advertise. Look how much fun it is to drink that milk! WILLIAM NOTMAN & SON/McCORD MUSEUM

Around the world, businesses began to build factories and urged everyone to shop.

But by the 1920s, North Americans and Europeans were buying less. In the United States, people often wanted to work fewer hours and spend more time with their families…which was bad news for factory owners (who worried about losing money) and religious leaders (who worried that, with too much time on their hands, people would start behaving badly—drinking too much alcohol and doing "the devil's work").

Factory owners soon came up with a solution. Every year they changed their products slightly. They made clothing in different colors, or reshaped the windows of the cars they produced. Then they advertised the exciting new changes. (Advertising changed too. It was no longer enough to spread the word that a good product was available. Now advertisers aimed to figure out what people really wanted in life and tried to sell them *that*. In other words, according to the ads, a shaving cream wouldn't just help a man remove whiskers—it would make him more attractive, make his life easier and maybe even find him the perfect wife!) Last year's fashions became an embarrassment, and people eagerly bought new products to show how modern they were. *Planned obsolescence*—designing something that will become unfashionable or will break within a short period of time—gave factory workers plenty to do. Advertising made sure folks worked harder so they could afford to replace belongings even before they wore out.

CRASH!

Picture yourself pulling two trays of delicious chocolate-chip cookies from the oven. You and your best friend eat a pile of them with tall glasses of cold milk. Then you give a few to the neighbors who helped you fix your bike last week. Eventually your brother comes along, spies the last few treats and asks if he can sell them at the lemonade stand he's setting up. He promises he'll earn enough to buy ingredients for dozens and dozens of cookies. It's a good deal…if your brother's a good salesman. But if no one buys the cookies, or maybe he gets hungry and eats a bunch along the way, or if the neighbor's dog comes out and devours them all, you're out of luck.

Something similar happened to people around the world in 1929, but it wasn't cookies that disappeared—it was their life savings. In the 1920s, North Americans and Europeans were working hard, and for the first time in history, many were making more money than they needed right away. Banks were also lending more money than ever before. Some people used their extra money to buy fancy clothes or cars. Others invested in the stock market, buying *shares* (small portions of a company). If the companies did well, they would share the money they earned with all the owners. But in 1929, rumors spread that soon the stocks would be less valuable.

When a parent is out of work, the whole family suffers. In 1937 in St. Paul, MN, kids took to the street to protest.
ST. PAUL DAILY NEWS, 1937, MINNESOTA HISTORICAL SOCIETY COLLECTION, HG4.4 P5 K

My Two Cents' Worth

When I began my bike trip across Canada in 2000, I had four bags of gear. I soon realized that I didn't need so much stuff. For one thing, I hardly ever used my camp stove because when people learned that I was pedaling all that way, they almost always invited me over for supper, let me sleep in a spare room and cooked me breakfast the next morning. Halfway across the country, I sent home two of my bags. And boy, was I grateful for that decision when I reached the mountains of Cape Breton near the end of my trip!

After the first few weeks of cycling, I sent home or gave away anything I didn't want to carry.
MICHELLE MULDER

YOUR VICTORY GARDEN
counts more than ever!

Grow carrots! Help win the war! War uses up lots of resources, and so this 1945 poster encouraged American families to grow their own food. MORLEY, HUBERT/UNT DIGITAL LIBRARY

Investors panicked and most tried to sell their stocks. Companies didn't have enough money to pay all the investors at once, and so the stock market in New York crashed. Penniless, businesses closed without paying a cent to the people who had invested in them. One in every four Americans was out of a job. For the ten years of the Great Depression, people tried to use as little money as possible. They made clothing out of curtains and grew their own food. Often, kids went without shoes, books and other things that families could no longer afford.

In 1939, World War II began. Governments in several countries asked citizens to save as many resources as possible to help with the war effort. In both North America and Europe, scrap metal got banged into airplanes. Bacon grease was used to make bombs. Families didn't have much money, but almost everyone had some material or skill to offer. They shared what they had within their communities and with the government, united in their common goal to defeat "the enemy."

A MALL IN THE LIVING ROOM

Imagine having been poor for years, or maybe your whole life, and suddenly earning plenty of money. After World War II, the countries involved gradually recovered. Most families had at least one person working at a paid job, and more than ever before, people in North America and Europe had extra money to spend. They also had new things to spend it on, like cars, bigger houses, televisions and all the products that televisions advertised. By the 1950s, folks were happily shopping again. Being able to buy was a sign of success, and families bought everything from frozen dinners to Hula-Hoops.

In the 1960s, people around the globe began asking how all this buying was affecting the planet. The more people bought, the more the factories were polluting the Earth. All this production wasn't sustainable, and small groups began to raise awareness about the environment. The first Earth Day was April 22, 1970, and the environmental movement has been getting stronger ever since.

These days, people with Internet access can buy everything from milk to plane tickets in the comfort of their own home. And we aren't just *buying* things over the Internet. We're also renting out what we have. *Collaborative consumption* is better for the Earth because we use what already exists instead of buying new products. This uses up fewer resources, which is good. But what if there were an Earth-friendly way to meet our daily needs and solve other problems at the same time? For example, not everyone on our planet is getting the food, clothing and shelter they need. And some of us who have enough still feel something is missing. Could a few new habits solve all these problems at once?

Shopping isn't the only way to get new clothes. These girls are celebrating Earth Day by modeling clothes designed from...trash!
JINLIDE/DREAMSTIME.COM

My Two Cents' Worth

What do you do with a broken toaster? Or a sweater full of holes? Products often don't last very long, and it's cheaper to buy new ones than to repair old ones. I first learned about Repair Cafés when I was researching my book Trash Talk, *and I was so excited about the idea that I helped start one where I live. We hold our events at the local library, and volunteers help visitors fix everything from jewelry to picture frames and many, many toasters!*

In 2015, some friends and I started a Repair Café here in Victoria so people could learn to fix small household items.
MICHELLE MULDER

CHAPTER TWO

New and Improved!

Here's a peek into the Medici bank in 15th-century Florence (now part of Italy).
LOOK AND LEARN/BRIDGEMAN IMAGES

FUNNY MONEY

How can you make a piece of paper worth ten dollars? First, you need to get many, many people to value it in the same way. And if you can get a whole country to agree, then you've got a new currency.

Money is funny stuff. As we found out in Chapter One, long ago people worked for useful goods like salt or sugar. Then people invented coins to represent goods because bits of metal were easier to carry around. Those with too much money to carry around could put it in banks. These days, in some parts of the world, instead of using bills and coins, we stick a plastic card into a bank machine, and the bank adjusts its records. If we want to know how much money we have, we can look it up online or ask the bank for a printout. In other words, adults aren't working for salt or even bits of metal anymore. We work to raise a number in our bank's records!

Of course, people want those higher numbers because the higher the number, the more we can buy. Being able to buy something gives us power. Did you know that each time we buy an item, we set in motion a whole system of human activities—a chain of events that often stretches around the world?

WE DEMAND A BIG SUPPLY!

Picture the latest, greatest toy on the market: the incredible Zoomzapperoo! You've been saving up for months to buy one, and when you finally come home with the box tucked under your arm, Sam from across the street comes over for a look. The next day, your entire class crowds around you on the playground, and a week later, half the kids you know have bought their own Zoomzapperoos.

The toy Slinky was so popular in the 1940s that the United States included it on a postage stamp a few decades later.
CATWALKER/SHUTTERSTOCK.COM

Marbles have been a popular children's toy for hundreds of years. Kids and grandparents alike enjoy playing in Istanbul, Turkey.
GOGOSVM/ISTOCK.COM

Now picture a woman sitting behind a rickety old desk in a small office. She's the proud inventor of the Zoomzapperoo, and she's just learned that it's so popular that she'll need to make far more. (In business terms, she'd say there's so much *demand* for her invention that she'll need to increase the *supply*.) This is fantastic news because now she'll be able to buy more supplies and pay workers to make more Zoomzapperoos. And best of all, she'll still have money left over. *Yahoo!* She jumps up and dances around her desk. She's going to be rich, rich, rich!

PAYING FOR WHAT?!

Companies earn money by making a profit. (That's the money left over after they've bought materials and paid their workers.) The less they pay to make their product, the bigger their profit. Unfortunately, what's good for a company's profit isn't always good for its workers or the Earth.

Many countries have strict laws about work. The government decides the minimum age for workers, how long a

Child labor is common in many parts of the world. This girl was working as a servant for a wealthy family in India. BISWARUP GANGULY/ WIKIMEDIA.ORG

A boy rakes cocoa beans on a drying rack. Many children work for little or no pay to help produce chocolate for wealthier countries. ILRF/ROBIN ROMANO

workday can be, and how much workers get paid. Government officials make sure companies follow the rules. Making a product in these countries is more expensive because companies have to pay their workers much more than in other countries where the government doesn't pay much attention to workers and their rights.

Often, North American and European companies choose to make their products in other countries, where they can pay workers very little, can demand a very long workday and don't need to be picky about the age of their workers. In some places, children spend their days picking cotton for T-shirts that North Americans wear, mining for metals to be used in Japanese cell phones or making rugs that lie on European floors. The small amount of money that these kids earn will help keep their families from starving. And by paying these workers very little, North American and European companies can make more money every time they sell one of their products.

Governments in several countries also control how manufacturers treat the Earth. For example, some gold-mining techniques are dangerous for local water supplies, spilling toxins like arsenic into the groundwater. Canada has strict rules against these procedures, and so Canadian mining companies are very careful when mining in Canada. But when they mine in the Dominican Republic and Argentina, where rules aren't so strict, they pollute the water in ways that they would never dare at home! Environmental cleanup is expensive, and so some companies try to avoid it whenever possible.

MONEY TALKS

Scientists estimate that for every pound of product we buy, forty pounds of trash are pumped into the environment. Waterways are filling up with chemicals. Landfills are overflowing with garbage. The air in various parts of the world is turning brown.

Industries don't set out to destroy the environment, but if they refuse to pay for cleanup, this is what happens. SUGIYONO83/DREAMSTIME.COM

Not all of this is due to factories, but manufacturers contribute hugely to global pollution.

Hundreds of years ago, before the Industrial Revolution, people mostly bought things from people they knew, and word got around quickly about where sellers got their materials and how they treated others. (For example, if a cheesemaker used milk that he'd stolen from a neighbor's cow, no one would buy his cheese anymore.) These days, we buy things from all over the world, and it's hard to know which companies are kind to their workers and to the Earth. We certainly can't find out from the packaging! Can you imagine a cell-phone box showing pictures of a kid in a factory in India, almost falling asleep as he makes the tiny parts? Or an image of dead frogs in the pond where the factory dumps chemical waste? Some companies care more about their profit than anything else, but they don't want their customers to know that.

My Two Cents' Worth

When I was six, I saved my allowance for months to buy a certain doll. Our local stores had sold out, so my dad and I drove forty minutes downtown and stood outside with dozens of other parents until the department store opened. When the doors unlocked, we raced up the escalators to the toy section. I grabbed a doll and bolted toward the cashier. Halfway along, a woman snatched the doll from my arms and kept running. My dad ran faster, though, and snatched the doll back. Boy, was the woman embarrassed!

These were some of my very favorite dolls when I was a kid. MICHELLE MULDER

MORE OR LESS

Companies that treat both their workers and the Earth with respect have higher costs when they make their products. In order to make a profit and survive as a company, they need to put higher price tags on the items they sell. And that's a risk. Some customers won't be able to afford the products. And folks who *do* have enough money might not want to pay that much. After all, the less we pay for one item, the more money we have left for other purchases, and being able to buy as many items as possible is a sign of a smart shopper…right?

Actually, this attitude is part of the problem. We're so concerned about that number on our bank statement that we forget about how our purchases affect the rest of the planet. And all our buying is using up more of Earth's resources than ever before. Each year, we're using resources far faster than the Earth can make more. The strange thing is that some people are still hungry and don't have adequate food or shelter, while others have too much food and even too many things to fit into their houses.

WHERE TO PUT IT ALL?

Since the 1950s, North American families have gotten smaller and houses have gotten bigger, but often families still don't have enough space for all their possessions. One common solution is to rent space to store the stuff that doesn't fit at home, and North America is now home to over 53,000 self-storage facilities. That's the same as 38,000 football fields devoted to storing possessions that are overflowing from houses!

Why do people own so much stuff? And why do we hold on to it when we don't use it anymore? Back in Chapter One, we saw how people's attitudes toward our possessions have changed over the years. Cave dwellers didn't want to own

In many countries, kids make their own toys instead of buying them. This boy in Sudan made his own toy car. JOHN WOLLWERTH/ DREAMSTIME.COM

FACT SHARE: The word "wealth" comes from an Old English word meaning a person's "health and well-being." These days, wealth means having lots of money.

This isn't just a room—it's a whole house! Some families choose tiny, more affordable houses so they can work less and enjoy more free time. KIM KASL/BLESSTHISTINYHOUSE.COM

FACT SHARE: "To consume" used to mean "to use up and destroy." A few hundred years ago, no one would have wanted to be called a consumer!

anything that they couldn't carry with them. Later, families generally owned what they could make themselves. During the Industrial Revolution, people began to buy items that they *couldn't* make themselves. Money (as well as the stuff it can buy) has become one of the most important signs of success. And if we think of our possessions as a way of showing how much money we have, it makes perfect sense that we don't want to get rid of anything!

PAYING THE PRICE

Strangely, studies suggest that people with more possessions aren't necessarily happier than those with fewer. In fact, they might be *less* happy than those who have just enough. Some scientists say this unhappiness is a natural result of *consumerism* (when people believe in spending a lot of money on products and services). Manufacturers produce more and more products, and shoppers (*consumers*) buy them up as fast as they can be produced. Advertising suggests what to buy next, and consumers are always on the hunt for more and better products. Some critics of consumerism say that this ongoing search for something new makes people constantly unhappy with what they already have.

Other critics say that focusing on consumption, rather than human relationships, is the cause of unhappiness. Remember all those happy shoppers in the 1950s? The war was over, and people were making more money than ever before. (Also, for the first time ever, people could use plastic cards called *credit* cards, which let them buy things now and pay later. Folks have been shopping with borrowed money—and owing more and more money to the banks—ever since.) People could spend money on both items and services, paying businesses to do tasks that neighbors or family members used to do for each other. A family could hire a babysitter, a housecleaner and even someone to build a back porch.

The more goods and services people bought, the more they had to work to earn money to pay for it all. And the more they worked, the less time they had for friends, family and neighbors. Relationships with other people went from being one of the most important parts of daily life to being something that everyone had less and less time to enjoy.

A NEW KIND OF RICH

Environmental destruction. Poverty. Depression. People are working hard to solve each of these problems. But some believe that all three are linked, and that we can solve them all at the same time by changing our relationship to money and to each other.

What if we could meet all our needs while getting to know our neighbors and protecting the environment? Around the world, people are questioning the need to own so much stuff, leaning toward more sustainable lifestyles, and creating a whole new concept of wealth.

Volunteers in Toronto, ON, are transforming their neighborhood with creative ideas. José Ortega's vibrant art helps create a beautiful place for his community to share.
HELDER RAMOS

Getting together with neighbors can be a fun—and free!—way to spend an afternoon. RADIOKAFKA/DREAMSTIME.COM

CHAPTER THREE

Feeling Like a Million Bucks

EVERYONE'S SHARE

While some people in the world have so much stuff that they don't know where to put it, others have so little that they're not sure where their next meal is coming from. Most people do have other people in their lives, though, and together they can all make better lives for themselves.

If you've got the cash for ingredients, a lemonade stand can be a booming business. Imagine getting paid to sit in the sunshine with friends, talking to neighbors! MICHELLE MULDER

BORROWING A BIT

Ever notice how we need money to make money? That lemonade stand that your brother set up back in Chapter One, for example, wouldn't have been possible if he didn't first have the money to buy the lemonade.

When Fatuma Arawari was growing up in Kenya, her family barely had enough money for food. She had to drop out of primary school after only two years, and she never learned how to read and write. But as an adult, she learned about an organization designed to help people escape poverty. The organization

Zobeyda used a Kiva microloan to invest in a solar panel, which makes it easier and safer for her kids to do their schoolwork after the sun sets. KIVA

lent money to small groups of neighbors, and each neighbor took a turn using that money to start a business. For example, Fatuma joined a borrowers group and used the twenty-dollar loan to buy chickens. She sold their eggs, paid back her loan and kept a profit. Then the next person could use the loan money to start another business, pay back the loan, keep a profit and so on, until everyone in the borrowers group had well-running businesses, and the group could pay back the organization that had loaned them money. These days, Fatuma makes enough of a profit to put her three kids through school.

The organization that lent Fatuma's group the money is called the Grameen Foundation. It was inspired by the work of Professor Muhammad Yunus. In the early 1970s, in Bangladesh, Professor Yunus realized that poor people with great business ideas couldn't get started because they didn't have the funds. Banks wouldn't lend them money because the poor couldn't

Professor Muhammad Yunus invented micro-loans in the early 1970s, and families around the world have used them to lift themselves out of poverty. HOSSAIN TOUFIQUE IFTEKHER/ WIKIPEDIA.ORG

FACT SHARE: Professor Yunus and the Grameen Bank won the Nobel Peace Prize in 2006.

prove that they'd earn enough money to pay back a loan. So Professor Yunus founded the Grameen Bank, which offers *microloans*—sometimes as little as twenty dollars—to the poor. Financial experts told him that no one would ever pay him back. But 99 percent of people who receive a microloan work hard to pay it back on time, especially if the borrower is part of a borrowers group. (No one wants to ruin everyone else's chance to get microloans in the future!) Now several organizations offer microloans to people with low income who want to start a business. One of the best-known organizations is Kiva, which offers microloans in eighty-two countries. Since 2005, Kiva has funded over one million loans. Think how many people a little bit of money can help! Thanks to microloans, countless families around the world can now start businesses, feed themselves and educate their children.

Can swinging a hammer help get your family a house? Yes indeed, thanks to organizations like Habitat for Humanity that believe in sweat equity! WILLIAM NEUMANN PHOTOGRAPHY

Habitat for Humanity offers summer programs where kids can help build houses for other families.
WILLIAM NEUMANN PHOTOGRAPHY

SUPER SWEAT!

Usually banks only lend money to people who already have some money or valuable property. Most banks figure that someone who's saved money in the past will be able to pay back the loan eventually. But what if a family wants to buy a house and doesn't have any savings or property?

Habitat for Humanity is an organization that works with families that don't earn enough money to save for a house. So instead of money, these families start paying for their houses with a different kind of equity—sweat equity! This means that the family gives their time and labor toward the house, helping build it or doing other volunteer jobs for the organization. Once the house is built, the family pays some money every month until they've paid for the whole house.

Sweat equity is not a new idea. In fact, communities have been building with sweat equity for thousands of years, and in some places around the world, if a family needs to build a barn or a house, the entire village comes out to help, knowing that, when they need help, the village will be there for them too. Many hands make light work, as the old saying goes.

FREE THE CHILDREN

Remember the kids back in Chapter Two who have to work to feed their families? Other children around the world are raising awareness and money to make sure that doesn't happen anymore!

In 1995, twelve-year-old Craig Kielburger was reaching for the comics when a newspaper article caught his eye: *Battled Child Labour, Boy, 12, Murdered.* He stared at it for a moment, then snatched up the paper and began to read. Iqbal Masih was born to a poor family in Pakistan. When he was four, his parents borrowed 600 rupees (12 US dollars) from a local business owner, and offered their son as a worker to repay the loan.

In South Asia, Craig Kielburger met a boy who had never set foot inside a school. Free the Children works to stop child labor and help kids get an education. METOWE.COM

Many hands make light work. Up goes a wall!
WILLIAM NEUMANN PHOTOGRAPHY

Iqbal had to work fourteen hours a day, seven days a week, weaving carpets to pay off his parents' debt, but the business owner charged for food and shelter, and the debt kept growing. This kind of situation is called *bonded labor* and is also known as *modern slavery*. When Iqbal was ten, he learned that bonded labor is illegal in Pakistan. Two years later, he found a way to attend a special event organized by the Brick Layers Unions, and he told his story to the crowd. One of the union leaders arranged for Iqbal and several other child slaves to be released, and Iqbal became a prominent leader in the anti-slavery movement in Pakistan. His work helped more than 3,000 children escape bonded labor, but he was shot and killed before he even turned thirteen.

After reading about Iqbal, Craig learned all that he could about child labor. He talked to kids at school about it, and eleven other students joined him in his efforts to make child labor a thing of the past. Together, they wrote letters, made phone calls and organized garage sales and lemonade stands.

FACT SHARE: Around the world, one-third to half of all food goes to waste. People who catch it before it hits the trash bin can feed millions!

My Two Cents' Worth

Every few weeks in spring and summer, I get together with friends to enjoy an afternoon in the sunshine. We weed, plant raspberries, dig up leeks or move compost piles at my friend Chris's urban farm. Chris appreciates the help, our friend Mark and I enjoy learning more about growing food, and whenever we need help with our own gardens, we arrange work parties there. Building sweat equity can be a lot of fun!

Work parties are a fun way to get stuff done!
MICHELLE MULDER

Free the Children is now an international charity, helping thousands of children escape poverty every year. Schools around the world have started Me to We clubs that raise money for Free the Children. Making a few cookies, mixing up some lemonade and having a good time with friends really can help raise enough money to lift kids around the world out of poverty.

TO THE RESCUE!

Money is useful stuff. You can use it to make more money, or use it to buy everything from soup to socks. But often we forget how much we can do *without* money.

In 2008, nine-year-old Katie Stagliano received a cabbage seedling as part of a school program. She planted hers near her home in sunny South Carolina, tended it and watched it grow…into a forty-pound cabbage! What do you do with an enormous vegetable?

When Katie Stagliano was nine, she grew a cabbage that fed 275 people. Now Katie's Krops program teaches kids across the United States about growing food. KATIE STAGLIANO

Imagine walking through a downtown neighborhood, following a trail of fruit trees. Students in Los Angeles, CA, are turning that dream into reality.
FALLEN FRUIT (DAVID BURNS AND AUSTIN YOUNG)

Katie donated hers to a soup kitchen, and her crop helped feed 275 hungry people.

Inspired by how much good a single seedling could do, Katie planted an entire vegetable garden. Since then, she's grown thousands of pounds of fresh produce to help people in need. She also started the Katie's Krops program, which supports gardens all over the United States. Kids who volunteer learn how to grow their own food while helping feed people in their communities.

And growing food isn't the only way to feed others with very little money. In Victoria, British Columbia, volunteers for the LifeCycles Fruit Tree Project pick thousands of pounds of fresh fruit growing in backyards. They divide it among themselves, the fruit-tree owners and community organizations. And in Boulder, Colorado, volunteers for Boulder Food Rescue pedal to local markets to collect bruised fruit and other food items that vendors can't sell, but which are still perfectly good for making a meal.

FROM BOOKS TO BLENDERS

Ah, libraries. We can take home as many books as we like, and when we return them, someone else can enjoy them. But libraries haven't always worked this way. They've existed for 5,000 years, dating right back to ancient Egypt, and for most of that history, only members were allowed in and no one could take books home for fear that loss or theft would leave the library bookless. In 1850, the government in the United Kingdom declared that every city with more than 10,000 people had to use part of the citizens' taxes to support public libraries. The idea soon spread to the United States and other countries.

And these days, libraries aren't just about books. Other kinds of libraries are popping up around the world too. Toronto, Ontario, is home to the Kitchen Library, where members can borrow kitchen appliances like blenders, juicers and dehydrators

The Food Rescue program in Jackson Hole, WY, uses pedal power to feed hungry people instead of filling trash bins.
ALISON DUNFORD/HOLE FOOD RESCUE

Ancient Romans built this library almost 2,000 years ago in what is now Selçuk, Turkey. It was able to hold up to 12,000 scrolls.
BENH LIEU SONG/WIKIPEDIA.ORG

FACT SHARE: In 2006, Kyle MacDonald of Montréal, QC, was out of a job but wanted a house. He set up a website where he offered to trade a red paperclip for something else. Fourteen trades later, he had a house in a small town on the Canadian prairies!

Want to catch a fish near Sudbury, ON? Visit the library first, and they'll lend you a fishing rod! JESSICA WATTS

for up to seven days. It's not quite free, but at less than ten dollars a month, it's a whole lot cheaper than buying all those machines.

Tool libraries are also becoming more common, and so are toy libraries, where, for a small membership fee, people can have access to all the items they need without having to own them. This not only helps people in need, but it also builds community and protects the planet. Each time someone borrows an item instead of buying one, manufacturers can produce one fewer of that item. That means sparing resources and producing less waste. The more people borrow—instead of buy—the better off the planet will be. (Some people wonder if it'll mean manufacturers will run out of money and workers will lose their jobs. Chances are, it's not going to be a problem, but more about that in Chapter Four.)

I'LL TRADE YA!

Thousands of years ago, before money, people traded stuff. Even today, trading has helped plenty of families survive very difficult times.

My Two Cents' Worth

When my daughter was a toddler, a friend told us about a local toy library. I'll never forget the first time we went in. My daughter had never seen so many toys in one place before, and she couldn't believe she was allowed to take home any three she wanted. I explained that she'd have to bring them back in two weeks, but that didn't seem to matter. Bringing them back meant getting to choose three more!

Libraries aren't just for books. Here's one where you can check out toys!
MICHELLE MULDER

In 2011, a group of low-income women in Brooklyn, New York, gathered to talk about money. They soon realized they had a lot in common: most of them had suffered violence in their lives, all of them were worried about making enough money to survive, and each one had something to offer. They began to trade (or *barter*). Some women bartered food for a ride to work. Others swapped childcare for shoes. Their trading became the Black Women's Blueprint barter network, a money-free way for women to build community and meet each other's needs.

The world's population is growing, but most scientists believe the Earth can provide enough resources to feed and clothe every person on the planet. The trick is to make sure everyone gets a fair share. And as people in various cultures are discovering, spreading the wealth can be both easier and much more enjoyable than we might think.

Need something new to read? Visit a phone booth in New York City. What a perfect little spot for a book exchange!
JOHN LOCKE

When you want to build something, a tool library, like this one in Baltimore, MD, can lend you all the tools you need. PIPER WATSON

CHAPTER FOUR

Now That's Rich

THE MONEYLESS MAN

Ever wondered what life would be like without money? In 2008, Irish activist Mark Boyle decided to find out. He gave up money on Buy Nothing Day in November 2008, and he hasn't used it since! How does he get by? The same way people did long before money was invented: trading. He works in exchange for food, shelter, Internet access and other services, and he grows his own food. Instead of a bank account, he relies on good relationships with friends and neighbors. By helping others, and receiving their help when necessary, Mark feels that his life is much richer than ever before. He also notices that his lifestyle is less harmful to the Earth. "If we grew our own food," Mark says, "we wouldn't waste a third of it as we do today. If we made our own tables and chairs, we wouldn't throw them out the moment we changed the interior decor. If we had to clean our own drinking water, we probably wouldn't contaminate it."

Buy Nothing Day is an international day of protest against consumerism. It's held every November. LARS ARONSSON/WIKIPEDIA.ORG

Families in several countries have joined what Mark calls the Freeconomy movement, trying to avoid money while meeting their needs. The idea of living without money seems extreme and even bizarre, but if we look back over the hundreds of thousands of years that people have been on the planet, money is a relatively new invention. For most of human history, we've relied on each other just as Mark does now.

For people who know what's safe to eat, nature can provide lots of food for free! ALAN MUSKAT

THE SHARE SCARE

Of course, living without money isn't for everyone. Those coins, bills and plastic cards are very convenient. But even by choosing to buy fewer items, people can change the way the world works.

Not everyone thinks this is a good idea. Some worry that if people buy less, companies will run out of money and disappear, which will mean that workers lose jobs, and soon we'll all struggle to survive. That would be absolutely true if everyone decided all of a sudden to stop using money or to start buying less. But societies don't change that fast! Cultures and habits change slowly. And while they change, people and businesses adapt. Since humans first walked the Earth, we've been adapting to the situation around us. Right now, our planet needs care, and using up fewer resources is the most important way we can protect our planet. Better yet, by sharing, we also support people who aren't getting enough to survive, and we build stronger communities, which support everyone. What's not to like?

FACT SHARE: Buy Nothing Day is an international day of protest against buying more than necessary. It was founded in Vancouver, BC, in 1992, and now people in more than 65 countries join the protest by cutting up their credit cards, organizing (free) public parties or collecting coats for people in need.

FREECYCLING! WHEEEE!

What is garbage? If you ask Deron Beal, he'll say there's no such thing. What we see as garbage is only useful items in the wrong place.

That's what he was thinking in 2003 when he invented Freecycle to connect useful items to people who wanted them.

Imagine going to a market where everything is free! STACEY MARIE SKELETON KEY/ WIKIMEDIA.ORG

Friends and coworkers told him about their old mattresses, leftover paint, filing cabinets and broken-down bicycles, and he sent out an email to acquaintances who might be interested. Eventually, he built a Freecycle website and posted available items. By 2011, people were giving away over 24,000 items on Freecycle *every day*. Think of all the newfound space that the givers have in their houses, how happy the receivers are, and how many millions of tons of "garbage" Freecycle is keeping out of the landfill every year!

GROWIN' IN MY NEIGHBORHOOD

Garbage isn't the only problem that sharing can solve. Did you know that it can get you out of mowing the lawn too?

All over North America and Europe, people are sharing their backyards. Half of them are tired of hauling the lawnmower out every week. The other half would love to grow their own veggies but don't have the land. Together, they all get exactly what they want, with the added bonus of new friendships.

My Two Cents' Worth

We know everyone in our small apartment building. Most days someone knocks on our door to offer us strawberries, invite us over for pie or ask to borrow a muffin tin. On Sundays, our door stays wide open because my daughter and a friend across the hall enjoy running back and forth to play, first in his apartment and then in ours. Long live strong communities!

We chose our apartment because it's close to the ocean, playgrounds, the library and my daughter's school. But what we like best is our neighbors! MICHELLE MULDER

Want to grow food but you don't have a yard? Why not share someone else's?
MOLLY COSTELLO

You don't need much space to grow a garden. Even the grassy strip between sidewalk and street will produce a good crop of chard and herbs. MICHELLE MULDER

And yards aren't the only living spaces people have begun to share recently. In Deventer, the Netherlands, elders living in retirement homes complained of feeling isolated and surrounded by other old folks all the time. Meanwhile, university students in the same city complained that the only places they could afford to live were small, dirty and expensive. The solution? Six university students moved into a local retirement home. The students get large, clean apartments in exchange for spending thirty hours a month with the elderly residents. Jurrien, who's twenty, teaches eighty-five-year-old Anton how to email, do Internet searches and look up videos. Another student, Jordi, took a group of elders into the garden, gave them spray paint and cardboard, and taught them about graffiti! Surprising—and delightful—things can happen when people share space.

WHICH BOOK ARE YOU?

Have you ever wondered what it's like to be a police officer, a woman who wears a religious headcovering or a person who uses a wheelchair? Wouldn't it be great to be able to ask someone these questions?

In 2000, at a festival in Copenhagen, Denmark, an organization called Stop the Violence set up the world's first Human Library. The idea was to raise awareness about prejudice and to get people talking to each other. Visitors could choose from seventy-five "living books," and soon a policeman was happily chatting with a graffiti artist, a politician was talking to a youth activist, and a football fan and a feminist were deep in conversation. By spending time talking to people they might never have spoken with otherwise, participants began seeing each other as human beings, instead of focusing on what made them different. Human Library events are now held in countries around the globe, including Romania, Iceland, Finland, Norway, Italy, the Netherlands, Slovenia, Belgium, Portugal, Australia and Canada.

TIME IN THE BANK

Kids growing up in Gobols, a neighborhood of Glasgow, Scotland, are changing their minds about where they live. It used to be a tough, dangerous area. Most families had barely enough money to survive, and some turned to crime to make ends meet. But a new kind of bank is changing all that. It's a time bank, where instead of banking money, people bank time. For example, if you spend an hour buying groceries for an elderly neighbor, then later you could receive an hour of help with bicycle repair from someone else. Everyone's time is valued equally, and now people know who to call for help with just about anything. Better yet, they know that no matter how little money they have, their time and skills are valuable and can help them get by. In recent years, hundreds of time banks have sprouted up worldwide.

The Trade School network is another way to share skills, while building community at the same time. In over twenty cities around the world, people can sign up to teach something they're passionate about—from sewing to website design—and ask for goods in exchange. For example, in Vancouver, British Columbia,

Ever thought about trading your time and skills? That's the idea behind the time bank in Lathrup Village, MI. KIM HODGE

FACT SHARE: In 2012, many people in Spain didn't have jobs. Banking time instead of money allowed people to meet their daily needs.

My Two Cents' Worth

My friend Chris grows a lot of food. He farms at four yards in his neighborhood and harvests everything from kale to kiwis to lemons. (Yes, lemons! Here in Canada!) And everyone in his neighborhood knows about his passion for gardening. They bring him food scraps for his compost pile, and extra plants and seeds, and his local barber even lets him pay for a haircut with parsnips!

A haircut? That'll be three parsnips and a rutabaga, please.
MARIAN VEJCIK/DREAMSTIME.COM

Even a small balcony offers enough space to produce delicious vegetables.
FEDECANDONIPHOTO/DREAMSTIME.COM

one person taught a course on knitting and received tea and decaffeinated coffee. In New York, someone taught stilt-walking skills in exchange for bike parts and dark chocolate. Who knew that a bicycle chain might help you get a job in a circus someday?

HIDDEN RICHES

Around the globe, people are coming up with alternative ways to meet our needs and to walk more lightly on the Earth. The best part is that we don't need any fancy equipment to make this change. Simply by talking to the folks around us and finding out how we can help each other, we can meet our needs and solve environmental problems too. The more we build our communities, the more we discover opportunities that we'd never imagined possible. Here's how to discover some of your own.

Grow It!

A little bit of earth, a few seeds, some water and time can help feed an entire family. Even apartment dwellers can grow peas in a pot on the balcony. And neighbors with big gardens might be happy to share space in exchange for some weeding and watering duties.

A clothing swap offers something for everyone for free!
NEESA RAJBHANDARI/WIKIPEDIA.ORG

Borrow It!

Sometimes we only need an item occasionally, and then it sits unused for most of the year until we need it again. By borrowing—from a library or a friend—we get exactly what we need without having to store more stuff, and often people are thrilled to know that their belongings are being put to good use.

Swap It!

Clothing swaps or book exchanges can be a great way to enjoy new-to-you stuff. Ask an adult about local events that already exist,

and if you can't find any, you can always swap with friends or even start events of your own.

Sweat It!

Got a broken bike and no money to fix it? Why not find a handy neighbor and offer snow shoveling or leaf raking in exchange for bike repair lessons?

Use Kid Power!

Around the world, kids are feeding the hungry, saving other kids from slavery and helping build wells for thirsty families. Some kids travel great distances and pitch in with muscle power, and others sell lemonade and cookies at home to raise money for faraway projects. Helping out with something you're passionate about can make you feel like a million bucks.

Tell 'Em What You Think

We all need to buy things sometimes, and the products we choose send a powerful message to manufacturers. The more support we give to companies who treat workers fairly and respect the environment, the more likely it is that manufacturers will act responsibly. Writing letters or emails to manufacturers is another great way to tell them what's important to you.

PASS IT ON

When we grow food with our neighbors or receive new-to-us clothes from a friend or borrow a blender instead of buying our own, we know we're part of a strong community. Around the world, people have been caring for each other for as long as humans have existed. We've learned a lot about what works and what doesn't. Now, with technology like the Internet that brings us even closer together, we can create a world where everyone gets a fair share.

A Repair Café is a great way to fix up your stuff and learn new skills. To find one in your neighborhood, check out www.repaircafe.org MARTIN WAALBOER/ REPAIR CAFÉ FOUNDATION

These kids in Victoria, BC, aren't just playing hockey. Their game is a fundraiser so that other local kids can afford to play, too. MARY LUE EMMERSON

Resources

Books

Graydon, Shari. *Made You Look: How Advertising Works and Why You Should Know.* Toronto: Annick Press, 2013.

Menzel, Peter, & Charles C. Mann. *Material World: A Global Family Portrait.* San Francisco: Sierra Club Books, 1994.

Milway, Katie Smith. *One Hen: How One Small Loan Made a Big Difference.* Toronto: Kids Can Press, 2008.

Vermond, Kira. *The Secret Life of Money: A Kid's Guide to Cash.* Toronto: Owlkids Books, 2011.

Websites

Free the Children: www.freethechildren.com

Freecycle: www.freecycle.org

Habitat for Humanity Canada: www.habitat.ca

Katie's Krops: www.katieskrops.com

Kiva (Microloans): www.kiva.org

Me to We: www.metowe.com

Trade School: www.tradeschool.coop

Acknowledgments

I thought about this book for a long time before I dared put it on paper. And I may never have sat down at the keyboard had it not been for Erin Mossop, Mark Weston, Chris Adams, Susan Braley and Gastón Castaño. Huge thanks for listening to me talk, sorting out what I was trying to say and telling it back to me. And thanks to the Canada Council for the Arts for the financial support that allowed me to turn those thoughts into a book.

As I researched, many people were very generous with time, information and photos. I'm especially grateful to: John Locke, Biswarup Ganguly, Kim Kasl, Katrina Zimmerman, Nieske at the Repair Café Foundation, Gillian Hallissey at Kiva, Kim Hodge, Pete Moorhouse, Sudbury Public Library, and Mary Rose MacLachlan, who kindly sourced an image based solely on my misinformation about its origin! Thanks, too, to all those who were willing to appear in photos in this book.

Several books for adults helped me better understand my subject. Among my favorites have been *The Story of Stuff* by Annie Leonard with Ariane Conrad; *Affluenza: The All-Consuming Epidemic* by John de Graaf et al., and *Your Money or Your Life* by Vicki Robin and Joe Dominguez. Shareable (www.shareable.net) also opened my eyes to inspiring initiatives around the planet.

Of course, this book wouldn't have been possible without the fantastic team at Orca Book Publishers. Thanks for taking a chance on this rather unconventional topic. Thanks to Sarah Harvey for excellent editing suggestions, to Kelly Laycock for careful copyedits and fancy photo footwork, and to Jenn Playford for the beautiful design. What a team!

To my family and friends, who have supported me with everything from cups of tea to work parties, thank you. I'm so grateful to have you all in my lives!

Glossary

advertising—calling something to the attention of the public through paid announcements as a way to increase sales of a product or service

afford—someone's ability to pay for something relative to the price of it

barter—to exchange things (such as products or services) for other things instead of money

bonded labor—a person's pledge of their labor or services as security for the repayment for a debt or other obligation

book exchange—place where books are traded or swapped for other books at no charge

child labor—employment of children that is mentally, emotionally or physically harmful and interferes with childhood and regular attendance at school

collaborative consumption—the sharing of resources and access to goods and services rather than individual ownership, often coordinated through community-based online services

Communism—a system of government in which private property is eliminated and money, food and resources are divided equally between citizens

consumerism—a belief that it is good for people to spend lots of money on goods and services

credit—money that a bank or business will allow a person to use and then pay back in the future

currency—objects that represent how much something else is worth, such as coins, paper bills, plastic cards, or cowry shells environmental movement—an organized effort to address issues that affect the health of the planet, through sustainable management of resources and stewardship of the environment

Freeconomy movement—a movement aimed at creating a money-less economy, based on developing good relationships within a community that trades services and goods instead

Human Library—a place where real people are on loan to readers for shared dialogue as a way to challenge stereotypes and prejudices through conversation

Industrial Revolution—the transition to new manufacturing processes that involved replacing human labor with machines (from 1760 to sometime between 1820 and 1840)

invest—to commit money to something to earn a greater return in the future

loan—an amount of money given to someone with the promise that it is to be paid back

microloan—a very small loan (sometimes as little as twenty dollars) typically to help finance a small project by someone living in poverty to help them earn money

modern slavery—the system of human exploitation that continues today as a way to make a profit off of the victimization of impoverished people, often women and children

nomad—a member of a group of people who move from place to place instead of living in one place all the time

planned obsolescence—designing something that will become unfashionable or will break within a short amount of time

pollute—the act of making land, water or air dirty and not safe to use

possessions—anything a person owns

poverty—the state of being poor, or lacking something essential for a person's health or well-being

profit—money left over after all expenses have been paid

renting—to pay money in return for being able to use something that belongs to someone else

shares—small equal portions that a company is divided into and owned by multiple shareholders

stock market—the system for buying and selling shares of a company

sustainable—methods that allow natural resources to last a long time without being destroyed

sweat equity—someone's contribution to a project in the form of effort and work, as opposed to paying others to perform the task

time bank—a way of sharing skills and time instead of money as a way to build supportive networks and strong communities

volunteer—a person who does work without getting paid to do it

wealth—large amount of money and possessions; originally from the Old English word meaning a person's "health and well-being"

yard sharing—a local food and urban farming arrangement where a landowner allows a gardener access to land, typically a front or back yard, in order to grow food

Index

Page numbers in **bold** *indicate an image; there may also be text related to the same topic on that page*

Index